HO
JACO

EXPULSION FROM
PARADISE

PENGUIN BOOKS

PENGUIN BOOKS

Published by the Penguin Group. Penguin Books Ltd, 27 Wrights Lane, London
W8 5TZ, England. Penguin Books USA Inc., 375 Hudson Street, New York,
New York 10014, USA. Penguin Books Australia Ltd, Ringwood, Victoria, Australia.
Penguin Books Canada Ltd, 10 Alcorn Avenue, Toronto, Ontario, Canada M4V 3B2.
Penguin Books (NZ) Ltd, 182 – 190 Wairau Road, Auckland 10, New Zealand · Penguin
Books Ltd, Registered Offices: Harmondsworth, Middlesex, England · This
extract is from *In the Land of Oz* by Howard Jacobson, first published by Hamish
Hamilton 1987. Published in Penguin Books 1988. This edition published 1996.
Copyright © Howard Jacobson, 1987. All rights reserved · Typeset by Rowland
Phototypesetting Ltd, Bury St Edmunds, Suffolk. Printed in England by Clays Ltd,
St Ives plc ·
10 9 8 7 6 5 4 3 2 1

CONTENTS

Gone Troppo

'Well, how do you like it?' the young man at the petrol pump asked me.

'It' was obviously Cairns. I tried to explain that I had only just this minute driven in, but he didn't have an ear for that sort of prevarication.

'I've been everywhere,' he went on. 'Sydney, Melbourne, Brisbane, Townsville – I've seen the lot. And you can keep 'em. As far as I'm concerned this has got it all.'

'Well, it certainly *looks* good,' I said, as though there might be some other way of measuring what a town's got.

'No worries,' he said. And when I asked him for a receipt he said it again. Only this time very slowly –. 'No – worries – at – all –' – because in Cairns there – really – weren't – any –.

In fact you didn't have to be in Cairns for much more than a minute to see that Townsville was kidding itself if it thought it could seriously compete. It wasn't that Cairns was at all beautiful. Or homogenous. If anything it seemed to have less idea how it should develop – whether upwards or outwards, whether for the rich or the not-so-rich, whether for celebrities who were here to catch marlin or for beach-bums who simply wanted to island hop – than Townsville did. But it was spectacularly set and you could not mistake what you were here for. With the rainforests behind you, half-obscured by the mist that appeared to be of their own breathing, you looked outwards to the harbour and the Coral Sea and the Reef itself beyond. And you watched the Reef traffic – the planes, the speed boats, the passenger ferries, the cruisers entertaining party-loads of week-end scuba divers – in perpetual motion, day and night.

The hotel we chose to stay at, although like most of the new buildings in Cairns exceedingly ugly, offered the twin advantages of a large balcony overlooking the bay, and proximity to the two blocks of Esplanade where all the action seemed to be. There was a bustling youth hostel here, and several cheap motels and boarding houses, and a couple of fish restaurants whose tables spilled out on to the pavement and very nearly on to the roads. It wasn't Marseilles or Nice exactly, but there was an excitement in the air, a sort of marine raffishness, a suggestion of slipped moorings, albeit that the majority of people out on the streets were young – American and European college kids having an 'amazing' adventure, Australian students taking a year off uni in order to hitch-hike to the sun, professional unattached bums who wanted to laze around close to islands.

I would have liked to spend a few hours here, eating on the pavement, but Ros reckoned we still had plenty of fruit to get through; so we sat out on our balcony instead, chewing on coconut and listening for what was stirring in the waters of Trinity Bay, while behind us on our hotel television the State Premier, Jon Bjelke-Petersen, tried to bully his way through an explanation of what was wrong with the figures that showed Queensland to have the highest number of bankruptcies, the highest unemployment, and the highest budget deficit of any state in Australia.

What was wrong with them, of course, was that they spoiled everybody's fun.

I was out again on the balcony early next morning, watching the sun rising from behind the Nisbet Ranges, where Aborigines on the Yarrabah reserve would have seen it first. Fishing boats were returning, looking laden. Large white shapes, whose outlines I could not recognize in the half-light but which eventually turned into pelicans, cruised up and down, observing the fish leaping out of the water. There was no sweat. No worries. The seas teemed with breakfast. What the pelicans especially fancied, they took.

Joggers were soon out on the Esplanade. All around the sea fronts of Australia someone was running. From a satellite the country must have looked as though its entire perimeter was a moving tracksuit. On the horizon an island – perhaps Green Island – appeared and then immediately shimmered. Straight into business. The hawks too were not sure what they thought about this no worries stuff. They twitched in disbelief at the pelicans' insouciance. Ever since leaving Townsville we'd noticed that it was hawks that hovered over the beaches, not seagulls. They were a reminder that this was man's country. Lee Marvin came here for the marlin and threw back anything under 1,000 pounds. This was no place for seagulls.

After our breakfast – which differed in no essentials from the previous night's dinner – we took a Hayles Cruise to Green Island and Michaelmas Cay. I'd done a small amount of homework and found out that from the point of view of style, of Reef-cred, it was just about all right to visit Green Island. You have to be very careful when claiming that you've visited the Great Barrier Reef because not all the islands are made of coral – and you look pretty foolish saying that you've been on one that is when in fact you've been on one that isn't. In the main those that are closest to the shore, with the most developed tourist facilities, aren't; while those further out, often inaccessible and sometimes invisible to the naked eye, are. Green Island, although a bit too close to be exclusive, was acceptable on the basis of its being a true cay – that's to say an aggregate of coral and sand. I'm speaking purely from the angle of snobbery now; from the point of view of conservation, and with regard to environmental sensitivity, Green Island wasn't reckoned to be very acceptable at all. But I didn't know that at the time. As I didn't know several other things about the island which had I known might have saved us no small amount of grief in the days to come.

We sat on the upper deck of the boat where, like every

other passenger on that section, we had no option but to watch an American woman, whose name badge said MARIE, rub oil into herself. She must have been about fifty, dating from the last time that whiteness was considered attractive in a woman, and was going in still for the sort of half-awakened pubescence that made Debbie Reynolds famous. She was dressed in the way I remembered it upsetting me to see Debbie Reynolds dressed, in cute off-white hayseed shorts and a pink spotted halter top and a straw hat with blue ribbons. She had been pretty once – was pretty still, feature for feature – and had almost certainly been the second string moll of a minor mafioso. Now, with no hoodlum to watch her oiling, she oiled, in a Brooklyn accent – 'I need protecshun, honey' – for us.

I tried to look at something else. Behind me Cairns was receding from view. It had no elegance at all from the water. It was low and squat and indeterminate, and could have been mistaken for an oil refinery or a series of customs buildings. Green Island, though, which I had to look past Marie to see, was beginning to take the shape expected of a tropical paradise – a flat green saucer with a sandy rim, a sectional view of a spinach pizza.

'Would you do my back?' She wasn't talking specifically to me. If we have to deal in specifics she was talking to another American woman in her party. But in actuality she was addressing all of us. The American friend was just a proxy. It was in order that the entire upper deck might get to work on her that she handed over the lotion, turned around, arched her back, and held up her hair with both hands. Thus with nothing to impede us, we were able to oil her very slowly, starting at the neck and working our way down over each shoulder-blade, taking care not to miss a millimetre of damageable skin, lingering over every spinal stud, even slipping the tips of our fingers just inside the strap of her halter, so that should it perchance slide in the sun, Marie would still stay forever white.

'Hey,' she said, just as we were wondering about the band of her shorts, 'this suntan lotion smells like pina-colada. Anybody wanna drink?'

On the red plastic seats to my left a pale, fashionably dressed English couple in the black and black Joseph uniform of aggressive introspection, held on to each other tightly. By carefully keeping his eyes lowered the boy had not gagged on Marie's flesh, but now the girl was beginning to look sickly. I had to fight back a rush of loathing myself, for the nerveless distaste of the young.

We disembarked at the jetty, pausing only fractionally at the underwater observatory where they piped Tchaikowsky's *Romeo and Juliet* overture through loudspeakers to get you in the mood for paying to watch fish. Yet another American girl steered her boyfriend past the entrance. 'Aw no, not there,' she said. 'That's pure kitschville.'

It almost made me want to go in.

6 We spent a couple of hours on the island, Ros snorkelling,

I lying on the beach. And then we were back on the boat again, speeding across the water to Michaelmas Cay, where we were transferred to what they called a submarine, though it was only we who were submerged, through the glass sides and bottom of which we were able to behold the wonders of the Reef. And wonders, to my absolute astonishment – I who had the greatest scorn for underwater gawping – they turned out to be. Fish every bit as multicoloured as the postcards suggested swam by us. Fish as bright and as neurotically gaudy as pop singers. Shirley Bassey fish. Boy George fish. Clown fish. Harlequin tusk fish. Fish that were striped and fringed, bejewelled and ear-ringed, bearded and even caped. Batfish that were all cloak and no face, just a pout like Charles Laughton's. Banded humbugs. Mottled reef eels. Fish that danced. Fish that told jokes. Horrid stove fish. Even, in the lugubrious turquoise giant wrasse, fish that I would have sworn were Jewish.

And worse, far worse for my self-respect as a passingly sceptical citizen of the upper world, I actually marvelled over coral too. Precisely as if I'd just that very moment come screeching into the universe, I gasped at its variety, its prodigious size, its extraordinary forms and colours. We nudged our way through coral canyons, past infinite ravines and pot holes gaping to eternity. We saw cliffs of mushrooms – fungia acitiniformis – staghorns, flower arrangements, bath sponges, and giant brains, like the spilled cranial innards of one whole year's intake of Oxford and Cambridge put together. I found myself making noises like David Attenborough. 'It's a miracle of natural engineering and architecture,' I said. 'A testimony to nature's most inventive builder and creator both – the tiny coral polyp.' We sat, Ros and I, with our noses to the glass of the ersatz submarine, as fish-fixated, as reef-drunk, as Hans and Lottie Haas.

The idea even assailed me that I would like to be a scuba diver. I was a long way from home. Nobody need ever find out. I made enquiries as to the cost and duration of the course and was put off only when I learnt that you were expected to be able to swim first.

We were returned from the sub to the boat for a buffet lunch, prior to being dropped on Michaelmas Cay itself for the afternoon. We were a smaller and more intimate party now than the one that had left Cairns earlier in the day; some of those had stayed on Green Island or been whisked off to other reefs; we were now down to about thirty, most of us bent on some serious snorkelling.

I thought that for lunch people were in the main dressed too scantily. A beautiful but intensely solemn German girl glided between the tables of prawns and beetroot in nothing but three small triangles and a slave anklet in matching colours. Although she was only carrying a small plastic bag she was to produce five changes of triangle, together with appropriate slave anklets, before the day was out. An unfor-

tunate American girl, with thick-lensed spectacles and protruding teeth, wore something that looked like a cut-down baby's romper suit, which transgressed the bounds of what I think the women's magazines mean by the bikini line. And the two male diving instructors who were superintending us had stripped down to tiny green pouches. Altogether, between the excrescences and the triangulations and the stubble, it was hard for either of us to know where to look. I was relieved when we were finally let on to the island so that I could stretch out face down on the beach, leave Ros to play with the fish, and go to sleep.

It turned out to be an extremely noisy island. Michaelmas Cay was a protected bird sanctuary. Not even Jon Bjelke-Petersen would have found it easy to get permission to build a five-star resort on this speck of real estate. You had to leave those birds alone. But nobody had contrived a way of protecting them from one another. They fought and screamed and exhibited all the other symptoms of paranoid anxiety that you expect of nature when it's left to itself. Except of course that it wasn't entirely left to itself, because we were there. Not that I was anything to fear. I scarcely moved. Every now and then I looked up to make sure that I could still see Ros's snorkel, then I dropped back down again. It was bliss having so much space to myself. Ever since Townsville Rosalin and I had been getting fractious and clumsy, walking into each other, talking at the same time, answering, 'Just look at that', with, 'Yes, but look at *this*.' A few hours doing nothing on my own on a coral 9 island, not looking at anything, was just what I needed, let the monotonous sea-birds – terns or whatever – shrike all they like.

On the boat back to Cairns Ros was all excitement about the fish she'd swum with. She'd made friends with eels and a sting-ray. She'd rubbed noses with baby sharks. She'd even cheered up a Depressed Gorgonian Crab. One of our diving instructors, Paul, joined in our conversation. I gathered that he was something else Ros had played with in the water. But he wanted to caution her against too relaxed an attitude to the deep. 'The sea is no respecter of persons,' he warned. (Now there were two of us sounding like David Attenborough.) 'The sea is unforgiving.'

He was handsome, in an innocent, soldierly sort of way, with golden hair and a trim moustache; but so similar to all the other diving instructors we'd come across today that I wondered whether, like the fungia acitiniformis and the staghorn coral, he wasn't yet one more miracle of polyp engineering. He claimed more conventional origins himself. New South Wales he told us he came from, and he had been in Cairns only six months. 'Though I don't expect ever to leave. Where else is there?'

None the less he still continued to harp on his theme of the dangerousness of the Reef. 'Your worst enemy can be yourself,' he said. 'Panic kills more people than sharks do. You must never panic – or at least, if you do, you must recognize it for panic. Say "O.K., this is panic. I'll give it five seconds." Then you say, "Right, Paul, that's it. Panic over."'

'Right, Paul, that's it. Panic over,' I repeated, to show that I had got the hang of it.

'That's it. Except that you wouldn't say Paul, you'd say –'

'Howard,' I said.

'G'day, Howard. Paul.' He gave me his hand. It didn't feel like a polyp.

'And this is Ros.' I said.

'G'day, Ros. Paul.'

We stood on the upper deck, with the breeze ruffling our hair. Behind us the islands of the Reef were beginning to lose their distinctness in the pale light of early evening. Dolphins leapt from the water. Reflections of banded snake eels and azure demoiselles still played in Ros's eyes. I was red from the sun and sleepy. A sudden gust blew spray on us and winnowed Paul's mustard-coloured moustache. When he asked us why we didn't stay in Cairns and scuba dive our lives away, as he was doing, I was truly stuck for a rational reply.

The following morning Ros discovered that she had a coral wound on her ankle. Coral wounds can become very quickly infected. The day before, on the way back from Michaelmas Cay, everyone had lined up to have theirs treated; the German girl required iodine dabs over very nearly the entire surface of her body. But Ros had not noticed hers then. We sat out at a street café and, while I read more details about the bizarre dog-eater, she bathed her ankle in Betadine. I could see that she was proud of her injury; that she was feeling good being an Australian again. 'If this keeps up I'll have scabs on my ears soon, with a bit of luck,' she hoped. I noticed that her wound excited the envy of passers-by also. You were no one in Cairns if you couldn't show that you'd been attacked by a polyp.

I helped her, hobbling like a starlet, to the car. Then we drove out of Cairns northwards, along the Cook Highway in the direction of Cooktown. We weren't leaving Cairns for ever, just for a day or two. Nor did I intend to try for Cooktown itself. There were problems with car ferries and roads, and I was running out of patience for any kind of travel that wasn't utterly painless. Daintree, where the highway strictly speaking ran out, would do fine. Any adventurous little folderols we'd fight over on the spot.

It was a wonderful drive; tropical forests, running between the coast and the tablelands, steaming high up to our left; on our right, miles of deserted beaches, and beyond them the reefs. We stopped for lunch at Mossman, the most northerly of the sugar cane towns. Since this too, though not to quite the same degree as Ingham, was an Italian town – the Di Bartolos and the Contarinos (and perhaps I just imagined the Figaros) were big here – I opted for a counter lunch of calimari and chips. Good, but not as good as what

Ros found in a shop specializing in 'Rare and Exotic Tropi-

cal Fruits'; granadillas and babacos and rambatans and black
sapote and carambola – otherwise known as 'four corners',
a fruit that resembled a starfish – and sour sops and, best
of all, custard apples. I fell for custard apples in a big way.
They were the only fruit I'd ever eaten that tasted like an
artificial dessert. They instilled in me a whole new regard
for growing things. Could it be that somewhere out there
was natural organic produce that had the taste of sherry
trifle or crème caramel? The question was only marginally
fantastic. Before we left Queensland we would eat a fruit that
had been specially cultivated to taste like pink champagne.

The Aborigines I saw in Mossman were not the confident
exotic islanders I'd admired in Townsville. Nor did they
seem to occupy the town in the manner of their brothers in
the Northern Territory or the north of Western Australia.
There wasn't that mute sit-down, as if by right, I'd grown
accustomed to. Things were jumpier here. They clung to
the outskirts of the town and generally kept their distance.
It was also my impression, as indeed it was Ros's, that a
number of them looked distinctly Italianate.

Why wouldn't they. We'd come across an Adolf Inkamala
in Hermannsburg; why not a Romeo Rubuntja in Mossman?

Half an hour later we were in Daintree – the end of the
line – a small slumbrous settlement with an almost sinisterly
enticing end of the line atmosphere. Probably no more than
about sixty people lived in and around Daintree but they
had only recently been at the centre of two intensely bitter 13

and highly publicized feuds. The first related to the creation of what the local Shire Council chose to refer to in its publications as 'That Road', thereby giving it a harmless tabloid-type storm in a tea cup notoriety. Whereas what 'That Road' in fact entailed was 32 kilometres of fiercely contested construction through an area of National Park, already itself unstable and having serious ecological bearing on the World Heritage Great Barrier Reef Marine Park. Its ostensible purpose was to link Cape Tribulation to Bloomfield, thereby completing the coastal route between Cooktown and Cairns; though it didn't escape the notice of conservationists (a) that other adequate roads already existed, and (b) that the main advantage of this one would be the provision of access to valuable chunks of real estate. They sat down in front of bulldozers in large numbers, and in large numbers were arrested. 'The actions of protestors, although determined,' the Shire Council pamphlet in my possession crowed, 'proved to be of little more than nuisance value, and failed to delay the project.' 'That Road' went through, large tracts of rare coastal rainforest came down, and the community was left divided.

In the meantime Daintree had become a sort of sanctuary and reliquary that pilgrims such as Carlos from the Peace Train had to visit – 'I just can't wait to get up there and, you know, just suss its vibes,' he'd told me – a pagan holy place, a shrine for wilderness freaks and tree-worshippers. Amongst whom, now that I had done obeisance through the windows of a submarine to the Tritons, I was prepared to number myself.

The second cause of even still more recent ill-feeling in Daintree was the eighteen-foot crocodile in whose belly only the fingernails of his female victim had been found. We'd read about the case in the newspapers while we were still in England, but we came to hear some of its more frightful details from one of the actors in the ensuing drama, an urbane middle-aged European with a polished forehead and a gold chain around his neck, who ran the Daintree souvenir shop and had spoken out against the wanton destruction of crocodiles which had followed the accident. Why blame them? he had asked. The crocs were just being crocs, doing what any croc would do. Anyone fooling about in that river, known to be infested with crocodiles, was asking for trouble. 'I'd been out in it after a party myself, only a few days before,' he told us. 'A few of us had gone for a swim. I was the last. It's a known fact that a crocodile will only ever take the last person in a group. I suddenly became frightened. I had bad feelings. I knew I had to get out of that water fast. Drunk as I was I knew I shouldn't have been in there. If anything had got me it would have been entirely my own fault.'

Beryl Wruck hadn't been swimming. She'd simply been larking about on the jetty after a barbecue. She had a drink in her hand. And a few of her friends were by her. It was low tide and maybe her feet were in an inch or so of river on the bottom steps of the jetty. Then there was a sudden violent agitation of water, though not a sound from the woman, and that was the last anyone saw of her until her fingernails showed up three weeks later.

The shooting began early the very next morning, men arriving from miles around with guns and rifles. Ready to shoot up anything in the river that moved. They called themselves the 'Daintree vigilantes'. By the time the patrols had finished – and the night-time ones had been especially exciting, full of wild talk and booze – upwards of twenty crocodiles had been accounted for.

The man at the souvenir shop had not been the only one to raise his voice against the slaughter. 'It divided the town down the middle,' he said. The old hands against the new. I knew the scenario. I knew how the sides would have fallen out in North Cornwall. 'There was even talk one night,' he said, 'of them lynching me. But that was just drink.'

The drinking would have been going on at the general store that doubled as the bar. It was the owner of the store, David Martin, who had been the boyfriend of Beryl Wruck, and the main instigator of the violence. 'We still don't speak. But it doesn't bother me. We never really mixed with them.'

David Martin himself became something of a national celebrity for a while. A sort of anti-Crocodile Dundee. He appeared on television explaining how he simply liked killing crocodiles. He boasted of his exploits during the building of 'That Road', when he attached himself to the police force, free of charge, and spent a week plucking Greenies out of the trees they wanted to save. Returning to the croc killings, he explained to a newspaper that 'People were screaming for someone to show honesty and guts. We are just little old country boys doing the right thing.'

The rhythm reminded me of something. It was the poem that Rod Drummond had showed me in Derby:

> We don't pay no taxes, we don't make de goods
> Just real little Abos, way back in de woods.

To make the brew even stronger there were now drug trafficking problems in Daintree also. The body found on the Upper Daintree Road with shotgun wounds in its chest and heroin in its pockets was definitely not the victim of a crocodile.

'Well, this seems a nice sort of place,' I said to Ros. 'Why don't we stay the night?'

As if she could never sup on too many horrors, the woman who ran the caravan park greeted us with a wide-eyed, panting expectation. While she showed us around a couple of on-site vans she frisked us visually, for guns or microphones. I thought she looked quite disappointed when she found only a notebook in my top pocket.

I called on her, in her office, a little later to see if she had a corkscrew, but she was busy with other guests so her husband dealt with me. Surprised by the business they were doing, off season, I asked if the publicity had increased tourism. 'First there was the rainforest affair,' he said, 'then the croc topped it off.'

Our eyes met briefly over the ghoulishness of human nature. 'But it'd be a pity if the place got spoiled,' he said.

I decided not to press on with this. I felt that my curiosity as to the degree of other people's morbidity was a form of morbidity in itself. I asked him for a corkscrew and when he said he didn't have one I joked that he didn't look teetotal. 'I'm not,' he said. 'I'm a confirmed alcoholic. The only way I can handle the stuff is to stay away from it altogether.'

More wildness. More teetering on the brink. I stumbled back to the caravan thinking what a spectacularly steamy spot Daintree was, and how you could actually smell in the trees the knowledge that there was only one way in and one way out.

The river – That River – was just visible from our back window. In the early evening we walked down to it through the camping ground, past a man in a pure white Balinese shirt chanting a simplified mantra. We stood on the jetty, where there was a sign warning us to beware the very things we'd come to see. And where a couple of steel passenger boats, finished with business for the day, were moored. We strolled along the bank, warily, watching for sudden movements in the water, mistaking bits of floating twig or debris for snouts.

The river wound through country which reminded me,

in this season and at this time of evening, of Devon. High, lush and confidently various. But it was the greeny-grey of the river itself, its still menace, that told you you were a long way from Chulmleigh and Totnes. That and the mosquitoes and the sea eagles and the thundering of lizards' feet in the undergrowth. We stayed down there longer than we should, and strayed too close to the water, half mesmerized by the danger. Then we climbed back up the grassy bank to the caravan park.

Outside the office a couple of soft-voiced desperadoes on motorbikes were conferring about camp prices. One of them was Irish and spoke with a chilling melodious lilt. I remember the play *Night Must Fall*, and the use it made of the song 'Danny Boy', associating murder with mellifluence. The Irish boy thought $2.50 was quite a bit to pay for a strip of grass to unfurl his sleeping roll on. 'Do you get a shower and toilet block for that?' he wanted to know. The woman with the wild expectant stare X-rayed his saddle bags. And seemed to like what she saw. Instead of telling them to go somewhere else, a million miles from here, she was intent on making them feel at home. 'Of course you do,' she said. 'How far into the bush do you think you've come?'

She smiled at me, as I was passing. I smiled back, quickly and faintly. I didn't want the inadequates on the bikes to think I was smiling at them.

We stood outside our caravan and watched the sky go   19

pink over the Dagmar Ranges. Palm leaves swayed and creaked against parked vehicles. The undergrowth began to stir. We waited until the last reflection of light had gone from the evil river, then we went inside.

Just before bedtime, from a house that couldn't have been very far away, we heard the sounds of an electric organ. It gave us 'Beautiful Day' three times, a few tunes I didn't recognize, and finished up with 'You Are My Sunshine'. After that the sounds of the tropical rainforests took over. Piercing screams of living things in anguish in the trees. I'd heard that crocodiles made barking noises, and I lay awake a long time listening, wondering if there was any reason to suppose that one wouldn't come out of the water and head in the direction of our on-site van. There was only a flimsy catch on our door. Not one that would keep out the Irish motor-cyclist either. I went to sleep at last entrusting my fate to chance, unable to tolerate any longer the sounds of Nature's nightly tearing of itself apart.

In the morning we took a safari cruise down the Daintree River. Us and about twenty other people: a motley collection including three smart-talking kids from Sydney Uni; a middle-aged couple from Melbourne (he silent, she vibrant) and their fat, comatose daughter; a handsome and sophisticated American/Japanese pair, neither carrying a camera; and a discordantly blue collar family from Port Kembla, comprising a fleshly pouting wife, a fleshly pouting baby, and a tattooed husband in a blue singlet who turned out to know more about birds, plants and crocodiles than any of us except David, our guide and captain.

Carefully controlled and bearded, a judicious weigher of every statement and emotion, a man who at all times gave the impression of someone who had come up here to get away from people but still hadn't got far away enough, David had clearly not been on the side of those who pulled Greenies out of trees and pumped bullets into crocodiles. That the two issues were intimately related he didn't at all doubt; according to him, those who had lined up on one side of the first lined up identically for the second. To chop or not to chop, to shoot or not to shoot – they came down to more or less the same thing. He was full of passions about all that had catapulted sleepy little Daintree into public prominence, but he was weary of it too. Every day he had to answer questions such as ours, and every day he had to look away when he passed the other faction in the street – except that Daintree didn't have a street.

The botany was what really interested him. He would steer the tin boat towards the bank having discerned a single pale blue flower or purple berry that hadn't been there the day before. To my eyes it wasn't there today either. I couldn't keep up with him. I simply couldn't *see* what he saw. And, when I could, I couldn't like it. It was good to be back in pandanus country again, for all that the pandanus here was of the climbing variety, like everything else in the fiercely competitive world of the rainforest, a clamberer and leap-frogger. And I formed a special attachment to the egrets with their question mark heads and necks – a perfect shape for all Australians, I thought; one that would sort perfectly with their inflexions. But the rest was all brutality; one long tale of parasitism and strangulation. 'That's Wait-a-while, otherwise known as Lawyer Cane, because once you become entangled in its hooks . . . And that over there is a strangler fig . . .' Throttling. Suffocation. Death by mangrove. It was pure Darwinism out there. It was like being back in England.

And at last, to cap it all – to top it off, as the man at the caravan park put it – we found our crocodile. A twelve- or fourteen-foot brute that had done well to escape the slaughter, sunbathing on a muddy bank with its jaws open. What is the fascination with creatures that can saw you in half in seconds? We steered as close as we could and stared and stared. And then a little while later we found a baby one – 'Ah!' everybody said – and we stared again.

He grew lyrical, David, on our return to the jetty, describing the sights and sounds he loved most on this murderous river. 'My favourite is the Orange Footed Jungle Fowl, otherwise known as the large-footed mound builder,' he said. 'It has a lovely melancholy call.' His eyes went misty, his voice actually trailed off in a melancholy way itself, just recalling it. 'Very much the sound of the Daintree rainforest, I always think.'

I envied him. He is a lucky man who can hear a sweet

plangency in the furious life and death struggle of a tropical rainforest.

Before we left the boat a little mute contest was fought out between that not so *rara avis*, the bright-as-a-button Sydney Uni student, and the fat comatose girl from Melbourne, the latter having for too long now allowed the boyfriend of the Sydney student to feast his eyes upon the creamy softness of her idle inner thigh. Ostensibly the girl from Sydney was only showing affection to her lover, putting an arm around his shoulder and letting her hair caress his cheek. But I had learnt a few lessons on the Daintree River. I now knew a strangler fig when I saw one.

Expulsion from Paradise

The plan was to spend some time – one whole day and a night would do – back on Green Island. Whatever else we could squeeze into our rapidly contracting itinerary, Ros was determined to have one last snorkel. She had made friends with many of those fish. She wanted to see them again. As this was not a suitable island day we made a booking for the next. Then we drove back to Mossman to stock up with custard apples, took a look around Port Douglas, where we found Diane Cilento's restaurant closed but a frolicsome Bavarian coffee shop open and for sale, and turned up at Hartley's Creek Zoo in good time to catch the famous crocodile attack show and otherwise enjoy 'North Queensland's unique wildlife in a lush tropical setting, alongside a real crocodile inhabited creek and Australia's only walk-in dingo enclosure'.

It was here, incidentally, that I received my first and only serious wound of the entire journey. I was bitten. Just below the left knee, by a goose.

None of the animals at Hartley's Creek Zoo went in for being welcoming. Crocs of all sizes hid in the mud behind wire fences, trying to look like old logs. Dingoes prowled their walk-in enclosures. The cassowaries – yes, cassowaries at last – looked murderous. And the geese bit. This might have had something to do with the general scruffiness of their environment. 'Lush' and 'tropical' though the zoo was, it was also cramped and dingy. Or it might have been that they resented having drawn the short straw and landed in a performance park rather than in any of the more conventional forms of captivity. Hard as this would have been for the children of the Tablelands Dance Academy to believe, it appeared that there were some animals who didn't find their ultimate fulfilment in vaudeville.

The show proper began at 3 p.m., when someone who wasn't the 'Most Experienced and Entertaining Guide in Australia' as pictured on our brochure, but a self-confessed, though highly Australianized Pom called Peter said 'G'day', and pretended to go through the roof when we didn't, with sufficient enthusiasm, say 'G'day, Peter' back. He was an outdoor performer, softly bearded, with a highly articulated bush slouch. Culturally too he had far more in common with the eco-religionists who had set up stalls at the Expo, people like the Tablelands branch members of SGAP – the Society for Growing Australian Plants. The bus drivers we'd encountered in the early stages of our journey had all been individual survivalists; social Darwinists; existentially speaking they came fitted out with jutting jaws and roo-bars. Whereas Peter's allegiances were wholly to the Great Chain of Being theory, currently re-vamped into the idea of the planet as a giant and mutually beneficial allotment. 'We've pushed the croc back all the way from Bundaberg,' he told us, as he climbed into their enclosure. 'Now all he's got is north of Cairns. It's not much and we should leave him with it. For our sake as well as his. If there was no reason for there to be crocs, crocs wouldn't be here. Crocs are here because they're needed. If we didn't have crocs we wouldn't have barramundi. If we didn't have barramundi . . .' And so on, until there was a providence in the fall of a megapode.

As crocodile attack shows go, there was no reason to suppose this wasn't a good one. He prodded a few twelve-footers, lying invisible in twenty inches of stagnant water, into rearing up and showing us their teeth. By means of a large piece of meat on the end of a very long rope he enticed the meanest croc in the place – an eighteen-footer this one – into a simulated death roll – the method whereby, prior to ingestion, the croc subaqueously subdues his victim. And altogether he put on a convincing demonstration – should anyone have needed to be convinced – of why an Australian crocodile was to the human body what an American Baha'i was to the human nervous system.

Nevertheless he confessed himself to be even more frightened of the cassowary. 'Don't be fooled,' he warned us, 'these birds are accomplished killers. Just north of here is a creek called Cassowary Creek. So named because it was there that a cassowary killed three dogs and a boy in a single encounter. It's the toe that does the damage – that thing, there, that looks like a scimitar.'

I wasn't interested in any of that. Lethal animals are ten a penny. Even geese would kill you if they could. What impressed me about the cassowary was its digestive system. No messing about with gastric juices here. As soon as the bird had tossed down his apples and bananas whole and unpeeled he went looking for rocks to swallow: small stones, pebbles, whatever was lying around – he wasn't particular. Then he'd go off on a short galumphing run so that the stones could bounce up and down and pulverize the fruit. Primitive, but according to Peter, highly efficient. Certainly we saw no cassowary looking dyspeptic while we were there. And the rocks and stones? Passed quite effortlessly through the system and lying there on the ground waiting for the next time. The cassowary his own little eco-miraculous Great Chain of Being.

Before we left, Peter delivered us a small oration on the subject of wild pigs. Apparently the damage caused to the Queensland rainforests by unscrupulous developers was as nothing compared to the havoc wreaked by the wild pigs. 'They're not native, you see,' he explained. 'The Poms brought them in. I know – I know – my fault. But I'm not ashamed to say so. Now the politicians in Canberra won't let them be shot. That's the wrong kind of conservation. They're "monitoring the situation", they say, but by the time the situation's been monitored the pigs will have destroyed the forest.'

These were the only animals Peter spoke slightingly of.

I had no reason to doubt the truth of his diagnosis but I put his special passion against them down to their being Pommy pigs. It's common and natural for the English to turn against their own when they come to Australia. The country somehow shames you.

But for everything native Australian, no matter how low it crawled on its belly, Peter had nothing but good to say. Even the deadly taipan, which injects enough poison into its victim to kill it 118 times, he asked us to consider from its own point of view. 'There it is hiding behind a rock, minding its own business, and you come stomping along . . .' He pushed his bush hat back off his forehead and scratched his beard, trying to look like a frightened but otherwise well-meaning taipan.

It was a good try. It just didn't explain the 117 times over the odds the taipan poisons you for disturbing him.

It might have been for this thought that the Natural Order paid me back the next day on Green Island. Or rather – man and wife being one flesh until it comes to pain – paid Ros back.

The weather didn't improve. For the second morning running we walked out on to our balcony at Palm Cove and thought we might as well have been in Folkestone. A palm tree is a miserable-looking thing in the rain; as is a fallen coconut. The beach – no longer golden but dun-coloured – was full of them: wet and shapeless, like deflated footballs, or rejects washed ashore from some head-shrinking colony across the waters.

We drove down the coast to Cairns and returned our hire-car. We had only booked in one night as house guests on Green Island, but we were keeping our options open. If we felt like spending the rest of our lives there, we would.

It was an unpleasant, choppy boat ride. Almost no one on the upper decks because of the wind and drizzle, and not that many of us below either. People weren't taking any chances on the day. There were later boats they could catch. If it brightened up they would pack their five changes of bikini and head for the wharf. Meanwhile it looked as though we were going to have the Great Barrier Reef very nearly to ourselves.

There seemed to be a perfect circle of blue sky over Green Island as we approached; not so much a gap in the clouds as a sort of superimposition on them, an apparently free-floating disc emanating warmth and light. But either it was a mirage or a Will-o'-the-wisp, because no sooner did we reach the island than it was gone.

We'd been told to introduce ourselves to Mark, the Activity Officer, the minute we disembarked. 'How will I know him?' I'd asked the girls who'd processed me. 'You'll know him,' they promised. And I did. He was tall and dark and very clean – too clean: you could have eaten off him. And he was wearing a T-shirt which said MARK on his chest, and ACTIVITY OFFICER on his back. 'You must be Mark,' I said, 'I'm . . .'

He only needed telling once. Thereafter, wherever I ran into him on the island, he would ask 'How's it going, Howard?' or 'You right, Howard?' or 'Wanna join us on the reef at low tide, Howard?' The only time he didn't stop whatever he was doing to look up at me and use my name was when I saw him in the bar later that night. He was off duty then, I gathered, because he was not wearing his Activity Officer T-shirt. And he stared right through me.

Because our room, it was in fact called a 'Tropical', was not quite ready for us when we arrived – girls of several nationalities running in and out of it with fan-shaped towel and face cloth arrangements – we decided we would have a preliminary walk around the island, the cold and the soft drizzle notwithstanding. The beaches looked as though they'd had even rougher treatment in the night than Palm Cove. A few trees had come down and there was debris everywhere. We picked our way between it, determined to find marvels even amongst the ruination. We oohed at every shell; we aahed at every twist of coral. Then we both espied, lying palpitating on the sand, a brilliantly coloured fish. Perhaps an euxiphipops xanthometapon – a yellow face angel fish. What it was doing here, still alive, several yards from the water but with no apparent plans for getting back to it, we didn't understand. Ros, however, turned out to know something about resuscitating fish. It was the sort of knowledge that West Australian girls just somehow picked up. She lifted it gently and carried it in both hands back to its own element, passing it again and again through the water, 'to force oxygen into its gills,' she explained. I looked on, astonished. You can live with a person a long time and never have an inkling of what they know. After two or three minutes of this she knelt down on the sand and released the fish into the water. It made a spirited dash for the open sea, then, seeming to lose its nerve or its bearings, it suddenly leapt into the air, performed a triple backward somersault, and landed with a plop at her feet. I would have called it a day at that, but she re-commenced the whole procedure, running it through the water the way a child propels a rubber duck, all the while exhorting it with words of encouragement and affirmation. From the fish's standpoint it must have been like a telephone conversation with the Samaritans, so weighted in favour of staying alive was the advice .

And eventually it did the trick. The fish started to gulp and look positive. Its eyes bulged. It even wriggled.

This time Ros took no chances; instead of trusting it to the fringe of grubby surf it had funked already, she threw it high into the air, a great arc-like throw which made sure that sink or swim the sea was where it had to stay. And this time the fish responded. We could even see the channel it made, like a torpedo's, as it sped towards its future.

At the moment of effecting the throw, however, her hand had been cut open by the sharp edge of the fish's fin, and now it bled on to the beach. And also at that very moment, even before the fish had hit the water, she had heard the sharp, infuriated cry of a bird. It was a sea eagle, fanning the air above us, and looking to see what had become of its catch. Now we knew what the fish had been doing where we found it. It was the eagle's. The eagle had dropped it and was coming back for it just as we happened along. Now he would have to start all over again. He looked bitterly put out, only marginally avenged in Ros's bleeding hand. He glided low over us, giving us a glimpse of the lovely reddish brown of his wing tips, and an idea of how nice it would have been to have had him for a friend. I thought of the albatross. *And we had done an hellish thing and it would work us woe.* Or rather, Ros had. She might have saved a life instead of taking one, but she had still interfered in the ways of Nature. She had severed a link in the Great Chain of Being, and there was no saying who might suffer as a consequence of that. Was blood to be just the start of it?

It wasn't a drastic wound. There's a limit to how much damage a half-dead angel fish can inflict. And in normal circumstances Ros would have thought no more about it. But we had been warned countless times about the possibility of a coral-associated cut turning septic, and recommended always to go along with any injury to the Dive Shop, where supplies of iodine were kept.

We left the beach, the eagle still circling above us, and made our way to the shop. I sat out in the garden snack bar and grill while Ros went to get herself dabbed. At a table near to mine a party of workmen, on the island to build more 'Tropicals', were taking a tea-break and ogling the girls. The most voluble of them wore a T-shirt which carried the words TAFFY'S HOMES – WE'LL DO YOU . . . A HOME; and since he was Welsh I decided that he was Taffy. Though to call him simply Welsh hardly does justice to the sort of Welsh he was. He was super-Welsh, hyper-Welsh, orotund and oratorically Welsh – altogether too rich a collection of sounds and sentiments for this fragile little cay floating in the sensitive waters of the Coral Sea. 'Eh, eh, eh!' he sang to his men, as a pair of only moderately voluptuous Australian girls came flouncing through the gardens, braving the cold in their bikinis. 'Eh, boys? Look what comes here, then. When did you ever see such a couple of lovely little fruit cocktails as these?' His voice rose and dipped, his appreciation deeper than any mine shaft. Not since Richard Burton's funeral, I thought, could so much deliberated vitality, such lyrical lilting rhapsodical love of life have been assembled. Only here on Green Island it was assembled in the single person of Taffy.

Was Nature striking back already then? Was Taffy to be the price I paid for Ros's throwing back of the fish?

I went to see how she was getting along with the iodine and found her coming to the end of what had been a violent argument with the man who ran the Dive Shop. He hadn't cared for her tone. He hadn't liked the way she'd come 33 barging in *demanding* medication. 'I'd have told you iodine was painful and not the favoured treatment anyway,' I arrived just in time to hear him saying, 'had you not been so *pushy* when you came in here.'

There was a little tell-tale quiver still, although it was all over now, about the bottom of his face. Closet jaw. No man who is on reasonable terms with his own nature will ever upset himself calling a woman pushy, even if pushy is what she is. Ditto ball-breaker. That whole cast of threatening women from damned whores through to termagants has no more than a shadowy existence in reality; like bugaboos and hobgoblins they stalk a mental landscape. Ros the fish-saver had ambled vaguely bleeding into what she thought was a Dive Shop and Dispensary on Paradise Island – to seek a little medication and hire a snorkel – only to discover that she'd blundered inadvertently into the pitted continent of somebody's private terror.

It wasn't until we got outside that I realized Ros was carrying flippers and goggles and the rest of it not merely for herself but also had a set marked GIANT (this referred to foot size) for me. Given that I couldn't swim I wondered how I would benefit from these, but she was too angry from her encounter still to tell me. I gathered that I would lie face down in twenty inches of water – which was enough after all for an eighteen-foot crocodile to be content in – and at least get a look at the wonders of the shallows as a kind of compensation for missing out on the wonders of the deep. We trudged across the island, ruminating; past dripping ferns and drooping palms and signs explaining that this area or that area was set aside for regeneration and would we therefore stay out of them, until we reached the water.

It looked cold and inhospitable. Not the translucent blue of our previous visit but a dirty disconsolate grey. I stepped into my flippers and looked about me, hoping that no one was watching, just as the rain fell. Real rain this time, heavy gobs of it, not so much falling as thrown. From more distant reefs came the rumble of thunder. We trudged back to our 'Tropical', using one of my GIANT flippers each in lieu of umbrellas. We must have looked like bird-men in a Voodoo mystery play.

Once we had dried ourselves with the fans and flowers and conch shells which it took me a while to believe were really our towels, we decided it might be pleasant to sit out under our verandah, where there was a table and chairs, and watch the rain from there. We could read, put our feet up, catch up with our journals, write postcards, and otherwise contrive to squeeze some enjoyment yet out of the island.

This worked fine for about ten minutes, then we heard Taffy and his men returning through the jungle from their tea-break. Singing. Like the Seven Dwarfs. Ours was the last completed 'Tropical' on the row. Work was proceeding on the next one, ten yards away. I didn't mind the sawing too much. Or the hammering. Or the noise of the electric drills. It was the cursing I couldn't take. The *Welsh* cursing. Of all the inharmonious sounds in the world there can be none that has so little in the way of saving grace or compensating virtue as a Welshman shouting, 'Ohh, fack!' on a tropical island. Cruel anywhere, but too cruel here.

We stuck it for as long as we could, but the minute the rain stopped we tried the beach again. The same thing happened. No sooner was I rubberized than down it came. And we had to dash for it once more. Given that we were intending to go into water anyway I can't now work out why we were so frightened of the rain. But I suppose we chose to be the masters of our fate; we wanted to get wet our own way.

In this fashion, between Taffy's sonorous swearing and these fruitless flippered forays to the beach, our afternoon in paradise was frittered away. We buried what was left of it in Marineland Melanesia, a crocodile and reptile house on the island, run by a man who wore dark glasses and kept a coloured jungle bird on his shoulder. It was a rich, intoxicating collection of tropical excesses: creatures that grew too big, like sharks and giant turtles and of course crocodiles; and artefacts associated with overheated rituals from Papua New Guinea and the forests of Borneo.

Ros talked to the man with the bird on his shoulder; although like all people who wear dark glasses indoors he would rather not have talked to anybody. He caught his own crocodiles. Harpooned them. He wanted that to sound more brutal a method than it in fact was. It was just a small dart he used. And unlike the cullers and farmers sent by Canberra, for whom he expressed a consummate scorn, he didn't botch his job. They tried to catch them in nets and almost invariably ended up drowning them. He used his harpoon and brought them in alive. Just talking about it made him bitter. I couldn't see his eyes, but I stood within his field of electricity and felt the charge. He was bottled-up, pent; like the giant turtles which swam back and forth, back and forth, in their too-small pool.

'What'll happen if I try to touch your bird?' Ros asked him.

'He'll bite,' the man said.

Having a bird on your shoulder, I decided, was the aggressive equivalent to taking your mad brother Alfonso to a dinner party; it was another way of carrying your alter ego around with you.

We left him to feed his ravening reptiles, and since our dinner was still an hour or so away, and the weather had cleared a little and the tide was out, we took a long walk over the exposed dying coral, startling eels and small sharks in pools, and causing velvety pulsating clams to shut up tight on our approach. Only the star jelly fish, coloured the richest blue imaginable, were indifferent to us. And of course the coral itself. I'd been much taken by the brain 37 coral I'd seen through the windows of the submarine, but out here the polyps had created simulacra of the whole organic system of man; here was the large and small intestine, the gut, the heart, the soul, the seats of good and evil even – all in bright greens and flaming purples and lurid pinks.

After an amiably but inexpertly served dinner, we joined the other house guests in a stroll down the pier to the Underwater Observatory, where we passed a further hour fish-gazing. Mark gave us five minutes of his time each, sharing our port-holes and remembering our names. 'Look, Howard,' he said, when it came to my turn, 'an azure demoiselle.'

These were the last words he ever addressed to me.

Back at the bar a frenzied atmosphere was building up, because New South Wales and Queensland were playing each other in the first of the State of Origin rugby series and the match was being shown live on TV. Along with all the other guests, Ros decided this was not for her; but I wanted one more beer and something for my notebook. I soon saw that it was distinctly a staff-only venue. A place for the exploited to turn up after work and swap gossip and complaints. It reminded me of a bar at a language school. Everyone was over-tired from too many late nights and too much drinking and day-long duty rotas which were not sufficiently distinguished from social life. It was a sealed community, excited by rumour, rent with dissension, entire unto itself.

A Canadian girl with green eyes noted my presence with surprise. 'Most guests don't come here,' she told me.

I asked her why that was. She shrugged. Because most guests are boring farts, she seemed to want to say. Without exactly meaning to except me from that judgement. She looked sorry, actually, to have even bothered talking to me. She was attentive only to what was passing between the other kids who worked here.

I asked her how she liked it. 'Yah,' she said, 'yah, OK. Some of the people complain about the conditions –'

'The conditions?'

'Yah, you know – the state of the rooms, the amount of sharing, all that. But I don't mind. I'm only here for a while. Shooting through before University. I think travel gives you experience and teaches you a lot.'

I agreed with her. How to agree with people was what travel had taught me. I looked around the bar. A girl a couple of stools along was crying. A boy who hadn't slept for a month was rubbing his eyes and willing himself to stay awake for more. Mark had arrived, not wearing his T-shirt and therefore not obliged to remember who I was. And Taffy was there too, shining with expectation, ready for the rugby and whatever else life might throw at him.

'Of course this is not a rave island,' the girl with the green eyes was saying to me.

'No,' I said. 'No, I've noticed that.'

'Anyone seen Geoff?' she suddenly called out across the bar.

No one wanted to answer. She rose to go and find him, whoever he was. No one could be bothered to tell her that that probably wasn't a good idea.

I watched five minutes of the rugby, but my position as the solitary guest was becoming too conspicuous. And I felt a bit of a nuisance being there: a small carbuncle on the nose of everyone else's fun. Mark, I noticed, was not merely not acknowledging me – he actually disliked me. And yet only an hour or two before he had put his hand on my shoulder and pointed me out an azure demoiselle. Queer. I made my way back through the slithery ferns to our 'Tropical' where I found Ros sitting up in bed writing messages on the back of Green Island postcards. Within a week friends back in England would receive irrefragable evidence that we'd succumbed to the mindless hedonism to which they'd always supposed us susceptible, and were now blissfully whiling away what was left of our youth in a state of nature on a sun-soaked tropical pleasure isle in the Coral Sea.

In fact we left the island at the same time our postcards did. The continuing vengeful weather had something to do with our snap decision, the refusal of the staff to serve us breakfast, having kept us waiting until the breakfast serving hour was over, had more. On the coral island which we'd had a mind to disappear to dusky youths and maidens poured you coconut cocktails by night, and rubbed musky unguents into your city-fevered brows by day. We hadn't bargained on sulky treatment from kids who couldn't be bothered frying you a piece of bacon, so worn out were they from propping up the bar with Taffy the night before. 'We might as well be in Birmingham,' Ros said. I agreed with her. We dashed out of the dining room, threw our clothes into our bags, returned our un-flapped flippers to the Dive Shop, and just made it to the jetty for the first boat back to Cairns.

Also travelling with us was the Canadian girl with the green eyes. She was in tears and didn't look as though she'd slept. I took it that she'd found Geoff.

We didn't waste any time in Cairns, though the woman taxi driver who took us from the wharf to the airport wasted some for us. She didn't think we should leave town without seeing at least the outside of the new hospital. 'It's a beauty,' she said, 'really lovely, like an international hotel.'

She had a bad case of the rising interrogatives, so that when I asked about the level of in-house caring – 'Good service?' – she naturally assumed that I was making an assertion. 'That's right,' she said, 'that's what I've heard, too.'

By mid-afternoon we were 2,000 kilometres down the coast. If we were going to be made to feel we were in Birmingham we reckoned we might as well *be* in

Birmingham. Both Birminghams. The one in the West Midlands *and* the one in Alabama.

So we'd flown to Brisbane.

To tell the truth, apart from the amount of inner-city freeway (none of it as hideous as what loops around the Bull Ring), and the number of cops on every corner (none of them, while we were there, publicly pistol-whipping blacks), and discounting all the evidence of the brutal imposition of utterly unnecessary shopping precincts – for this was the place above all others in Australia where bulldozers were sent in under cover of darkness, like tanks, to settle the finer points of preservation orders – leaving aside, in other words, the personality of the Premier as graven on the forehead of his capital city, I rather liked it. It had a queer old-fashioned frisky air. A nutty exuberance which countless times caused me to laugh aloud in the streets. A country town like Perth, surprised by how rich how quickly it had grown, it didn't have Perth's anglophile sedateness. It wasn't remotely interested in refinement. It behaved like a hillbilly that had just come into a whopping inheritance and didn't mind who knew it. Looking at people going about their business or drinking cappucinos in the mall, I felt I'd gatecrashed a party that had been going on since somewhere round about VE Day, when coachloads of cockies had come whooping into town and been reluctant, ever since, to go back to their
42   properties.

The men had red faces and round chests and looked tickled pink to be out. You could see their politics in the broken veins beneath their skin, like an apoplexy waiting to break out. The women were a curious mix of bowling ladies with leathery complexions and sirens of the early talkies – Marlene Dietrich and Greta Garbo especially. I don't think I've ever seen elderly women dressed with such bad intent. Crones of eighty-five, wearing skirts three inches above the knee, shoes with deadly stiletto heels and open toes, and rakish white and blue bowling hats, stood in doorways of department stores at 9.30 in the morning, waiting for something to happen. There were old lips slashed with lipstick in every café, old legs, no thicker than my finger, in sheer black stockings riding every escalator. Pickled into a long preservation by the country climate, they were now content to go off rapidly in the city. It was like watching delinquency seize a retirement home.

A higher standard of behaviour was expected of the young. Outside every hotel were dress and appearance restrictions so complicated that you needed to check yourself out in a mirror to be certain you conformed. In the far north it had been sufficient to stipulate no thongs and no tank tops, but in Brisbane the texture of your trousers and the precise grooming of your hair determined your right to drink. Uneven turn-ups, too little ear showing, the wrong conditioner, and you were out.

Although there were reputed to be bars in town where 43

suspected hoisters were given the third degree, I have to say that we were never questioned, perhaps because we were together, as to the nature of our relational preferences. But in the lavatories of one hotel I did find evidence of Queensland's notorious anxiety about the spread of the spirit of the Gay and the Goanna. It was a stainless steel machine which offered you your own Germshield Disposable Seat Cover for a mere 20 cents a throw. There was even a little diagram explaining how you pulled out the tab and affixed it to the seat. If you left the tab on, and dangling in the bowl, the cover would be swept away when the toilet was flushed, thus ensuring that the next person would not be able to shield himself from germs for free.

Otherwise, though, there seemed on the surface not to be too much fear of what was catching. I saw my first ever Australian edition of *Pravda* for sale on the streets of Brisbane. I saw two on-duty policemen browsing through the modern fiction section of a pavement book-store, and after serious deliberation make a purchase of a volume of Frank Moorhouse stories and a new novel by David Malouf. And although I'd heard that some shops in Queensland wouldn't stock my books because of the illustrations on their covers (as some feminist bookshops, mistaking depiction for incitement, even in non-censorious London won't), I saw them shown prominently, one might almost say flagrantly and abundantly, all over Brisbane. As indeed I saw at last, in a section devoted entirely to the Australian contribution to the genre, the collected poems of Orianna Ooi.

There is always hope for a city prepared to make accommodations such as these to the life of the intellect in action.

We didn't spend long in Brisbane for all that. I made the mistake of dragging us off to see *Hannah and her Sisters* on our first night in town, as a way of getting Green Island out of the system, and it worked so well for me that it tolled the death knell over my interest in anywhere that wasn't New York. I came out of the cinema in a fury with where I happened at that moment to be. Queensland! Brisbane! What was I, as a Jew, as a European, as a depressive, as a gourmandizer of the quasi-kosher, as a connoisseur of social experimentation and disappointment – what was *I*, as a seeker after urban exhilaration, doing in Brisbane? New York was where I should have been. Not the real New York; I wasn't dealing in *real* anywheres. But New York as portrayed in Woody Allen movies – full of allure and illusory amenities, all Gershwin street-throb and dangerous conviviality, beguiling, trashy, tumultuously lyrical. So badly did I want to *be* Woody Allen (who was always wanting to be someone else himself), pushing my barrow-load of confused and disbelieving hopefulness up *that* hill, that I didn't just turn on Brisbane, I turned on Australia altogether and couldn't understand what had brought me back here so many times when it had so little that I wanted.

45

The truth of all this, of course, is that I wouldn't have felt any of it had I watched *Hannah and her Sisters* in Kalgoorlie or in the school at Areyonga, or even, had they had an outdoor cinema, a Tropicana, on the beach at Green Island; what accounted for my restless dissatisfaction was anti-climax – my knowledge that our journey was very nearly over and that we were back now in the Australia that had been long familiar to us, and which was indeed but a poor imitation of a poor American imitation of a European model. New York or Brisbane? The question never arose when we were chatting to the euros in the Flinders Ranges, or listening to the dingoes in Yulara.

As for what it was that kept me coming back to the eastern seaboard cities, even though they weren't New York, I was given a sharp reminder of it on our last evening in Brisbane. At the house of an acquaintance of an acquaintance I found myself sitting opposite a publisher I'd vaguely known in my book repping days in Melbourne. Left to my own devices I might very well not have recognized him. He was perched on the edge of his seat, ginger-haired and bearded, wringing his hands and looking arch, like a well-connected sprite. He *seemed* familiar, but I had been travelling for months and I was seeing what I thought were the faces of old friends everywhere now. So I needed him to say, 'So you're back then,' – as if I were a recurrence of some pestiferous minor ailment – for me to remember that I remembered him.

He wanted to know what I was doing here. I told him.

'Well if you're writing about Australia I hope you make it funny,' he said.

I pulled a face. I wasn't feeling in a very funny mood. 'Funny but not farcical,' I said.

'Why not farcical? The country is a farce.'

He poured me a red wine, although he was only a guest at the house himself. 'It's a nation of fuckwits,' he reminded me.

He took me through the details of Australia's national fuckwittedness. Its reliance on American and Pommy money-men. Its lack of an independent policy on anything. Its parochialism. Its fear of the Melbourne establishment. 'The only good things in Australia are happening in Perth,' he told me. 'Take Holmes à Court, who just happens to be South African-born. He's got the Melbourne establishment by the scruff of the neck. What he's doing to those fuckwits is the nearest modern equivalent to the Eureka spirit.' (That's Eureka as in Stockade, not Eureka as in Archimedes.)

I raised an eyebrow at the idea of Holmes à Court as a revolutionary, but he went on twinkling wickedly and pouring me more wine. 'Anyway, so who else have you looked up in Brisbane?' he asked.

'No one,' I said. 'Just you.'

He must have thought I was being ironical. 'You bastard, Jacobson,' he said.

A warm glow instantly suffused my whole being. I felt 47

as though a dozen little lights had been turned on inside me all at once. 'You bastard, Jacobson' – that was it, the very thing, the reason above all others I kept coming back. They were so damned complimentary, Australians. They made you feel you possessed such reserves of badness. 'You bastard, Jacobson.' Who else but an eastern states Australian was ever going to say that to me? Certainly no New Yorker ever would.

At the other end of the room I saw Ros looking anxious. She'd heard the word bastard and heard the word Jacobson and feared the worst. I threw her a mute signal that everything was all right, that I was getting what I always came for and could never get enough of: the ultimate male compliment, the asseveration of one's dangerousness, bloke to bloke.

'It's true,' I said. 'Anyway, who else is there to see in Brisbane.'

'You'd be surprised.'

'Surprise me.'

He did surprise me too. Any number of people I hadn't heard of for years – personalities, public figures, show folk, many I'd assumed had quietly passed away – were all the while living the good life in Brisbane, sitting on Germshield Disposable Seat Covers, and reading *Pravda*. But the most intriguing by far was the figure on whom Brando's part in *Apocalypse Now* had been based. The Mr Kurtz of Vietnam.

'What, here?' I found it hard to believe. I don't know

why; I suppose it seemed a bit of a let-down. After the Horror! the Horror! – the cannibalism and all the rest of it – you expected somewhere rather more metaphysically testing than the Gold Coast. 'Here in Brisbane?'

'Yep.'

'Do you know him?'

'I'm not saying.'

'What's his name?'

'I'm not going to tell you.'

'Why not? What do you think I'm going to do with it.'

He smiled and sat further forward, occupying even less seat. There was intense sardonic activity in his eyes. As if to imply, 'I know you, Jacobson, you bastard. I know what *you'd* do.' Which was the very thing I wanted him to imply. There was absolutely nothing I would do with any information relating to Mr Kurtz. The last thing I'd have the courage for was a visit. I don't interview men who've gone up the river. But I didn't choose to let my old publisher mate know that. I wanted to hear him call me a bastard again – just one more time before I left.

'Give me a little clue.'

He shook his head.

'His initials.'

'No. I'm not telling you.'

'Just the suburb, then. St Lucia? Fortitude Valley?'

'No. Absolutely no.'

'Suit yourself,' I said. I took my notebook out and

scribbled a few words on it. 'I'm going tomorrow,' I went on; 'I've got to have someone for the Brisbane section. If I can't have Mister Kurtz I'll have to have you. Publishers don't normally make for interesting reading, but I can jazz you up a bit. What was that about fuckwits again?'

The tense angles of his body somewhat belied the wicked twinkle, or vice versa. 'You bastard, Jacobson,' he said.

'Good to see you again, anyway,' he lied, as I rose to leave.

'You too,' I pretended to agree.

We gripped each other's hand firmly. It was like the locking of horns. In the old days I used to arm wrestle all my friends, and had we both been younger we could easily have gone in for a bit of that now. In the English-speaking world there really is only Australia where you can get that from your mates.

As we parted it occurred to me that I didn't in fact know who he was and that we might never have met in Melbourne after all. The more I thought about it the more likely I decided it was that we'd never addressed a word to each other until tonight.

Not that it seemed to matter.

We went on from this encounter to hear Hemi sing at the Port Office Hotel in Edward Street. Hemi was a nice, quiet, plump, bespectacled Jewish boy from Tel Aviv who used to be a tank commander in the Israeli army and was now the hottest rock sensation in Brisbane. I'd read about him in the local newspaper; how he'd turned up in Queensland three and a half years previously, supporting himself on a round the world trip by doing odd jobs, a spot of cleaning, some busking, that sort of thing, and then, virtually overnight, had become a pop idol – not anywhere else, just here in Brissie.

We had to fight our way through the crowds at the Port Office to get to the bar, and we had to fight even harder to get anywhere near the stage. I was surprised at how young the audience was. Given that Hemi's repertoire included 'Hava Nagila' and 'American Pie' you would have thought his fans would have all been my age. But no; he had found a way through to the kids of Brisbane and they cheered and stomped and did as they were told when he waved his guitar around and shouted, 'Everybody sing – I can't get no – o – o . . .'

The girls clawed the air. They pushed one another over to get a touch of his yellow pants or to tug on his Israeli beach shirt. He smiled at them benignly, a bit puzzled himself. He had tight curly hair and a double chin and reminded me not so much of the soft Jewish boys who were regularly beaten up in the playground after school, as their mothers. There was something comfortable and caring about him: something homely – *haimisheh*. It needed no imagination at all to see him in a *shaytl* with his arms covered and maybe just a dab of lipstick, blessing the *challa* on a Friday night. 51

Well, this was a Friday night, *shabbas* already, and we were in Queensland, sweating, while somebody who looked very like *my* mother, too, was slaying them with his Menachem Begin accent, and what his chubby fingers could do on a guitar. I couldn't get over it. It was too risible. But it was a good note to leave Brisbane on. It balanced *Hannah and her Sisters* nicely. Hemi proved, if anybody did, that the New York I hankered after – a noisy refuge for a wandering urban soul – was just a construct. He'd built his own – a condo with a busy view – right in the very heartlands of the most unpromising of all territories. As far as Hemi was concerned he was *in* New York.

Just in case there was any chance of my suffering a similar delusion, the young woman at the reception desk of the hotel we'd been staying at, the Carlton, handed me a couple of Brisbane horror stories along with my bill. We'd enjoyed the Carlton; it was a handsome wooden building with lacy balconies, large, high-ceilinged rooms, and a marvellous lounge in which we'd sat by the hour, watching Marlene Dietrich and Greta Garbo come and go, as well as marginally less elderly ladies done up to resemble tropical wild life – a banded snake eel, a couple of pelicans, any number of fruit bats, and on one occasion a cassowary, complete with a technicolour neck, a casque and, for all we knew, a five-inch lethal toe nail. Now, it seemed, the hotel was to be demol-

ished. The very best that could be hoped for was that the

façade might be retained. But everything else would go. For?

The woman smiled a slow sad smile at me and made a gesture which was meant to embrace everything that I could see going on in Brisbane with my own eyes. The preparations for EXPO – '88. And – it was vainly hoped – The Olympic Games, 1992. Like the rest of Australia Brisbane was caught up in a madness to pull down and rebuild – except that here the only things they could think of rebuilding to entice visitors with were malls and precincts.

'Not more shops?'

She nodded. 'Shops, shops and shops. And maybe, just maybe, a tavern. But no more accommodation. They assume people want to stay in Sheratons.'

'Can't the National Trust be trusted to take it on?'

'No. They say there's too much timber in it. It would cost too much to repair and maintain.'

'Couldn't they at least slap a preservation order on it?'

As soon as I said it I realized how naive I sounded. She looked at me as if I were a two-year-old. 'Preservation orders don't count for much in Queensland,' she said.

Well, if she thought *that* was babyish she'd heard nothing yet. 'Doesn't anybody protest?' I asked.

Looking back on it I can see that it was good of her even to have bothered to reply. But she did. 'You don't protest for long in Brisbane,' she told me.

She had, once. When she was a student. As a consequence 53

of which her car mysteriously went missing one night. When she rang the police to report its theft they said they'd impounded it for being illegally parked; and when she went to collect it she found it wrecked. Not our responsibility, they'd told her. Teach you not to park illegally.

It made her tired, just remembering the event. Creases appeared under her eyes where I hadn't seen any before. 'You get to find out what's going on,' she said. 'You get to know once the Special Branch are looking out for you.'

She was not the kind of person you expected to hear such a sentence from. She didn't look an activist. In any other town she would have been a model citizen. But over-zealous police – assuming she was telling the truth – can rattle the respectability out of anyone. And there was no doubt about the size of the police presence in Brisbane; they were everywhere you looked. Always in groups of three or four, often quite young men, lounging on street corners, privately amused, more trouble than the trouble-makers. It's my most abiding memory of Brisbane: boy cops hanging around shopping precincts, laughing.

We didn't fly out of Brisbane, as our ragged spirits might have justified, but hired a comfortable car so that we could take a leisurely look at the Gold Coast and chug down the Pacific Highway to Sydney at whatever speed we fancied.

I found that I liked (liked for other people, that is) the absurd resorts of Surfers Paradise and Burleigh Heads and

Coolangatta. Grant the desires and appetites they catered for and they made sense. The way they looked and what they were there for enjoyed a perfect harmony. People wanted to come here to see the sea – very well, they would *see* the sea. If that meant more and higher skyscrapers than you'd find in the rest of Australia put together, what then? How else was everyone going to get their own triangle of placid blue? Within the limits set by affordability, the Gold Coast was democracy in action. Everybody got a look in.

And the consequence of such dense high-rise water-frontage, for mere passers-by such as us, was an urban/marine landscape so surreal as to take the breath away. Stand on a beach anywhere between Southport and Tweed Heads looking up the coast or down it and you would see dreaming cities poised perilously on the last millimetre of land, impregnable batteries of luxury apartments rising like the topless towers of Ilium and shimmering in a sea haze as though they had no foundations but simply floated, like hanging gardens. Australian Venices for sunbathers and surfers, they seemed not to have been designed the way they were but to have fallen out like that, as if some freakish cataclysm had severed a metropolis, sinking one half and dumping a golden strand on the very doorsteps of the other.

There was sand everywhere. It was what you saw from every over-leaping window. It was the feature that concluded every aspect – sand, a roll of foaming surf, and the Pacific – the reward at the end of every little street.

It was in a car park by the beach at Surfers itself that I was accosted by a tired, lonely-looking man with cut-price tattoos on his arms who wanted to know whether the traffic lights up here had television cameras in them the way they had down there. He had driven all the way from Melbourne without stopping and in his fatigue had shot straight through a set of lights. Before I had any opportunity to offer my opinion he put himself on trial for this offence, appealing to me as jury, and insisting on his innocence. 'Actually it was only an orange light, and even then it had only just *turned* orange,' he said, relieved to be acquitted.

It was just as well. I could see that he wouldn't have had the money to pay the fine.

'So where are you from?' he asked me. He reminded me of someone I had once shared a filthy bathroom with in a mouldering house in Wolverhampton. He suffered the same blue-collar sadness and isolation. And he made me feel the same way; I wanted to kick him, then I wanted to bathe his wounds. He wore cheap trousers enlivened by a thick leather belt and a silver cowboy buckle. Had he been a character in a nineteenth-century novel he'd have said, 'Aw a muddle,' and not lived long.

'London,' I answered. I felt it would have been more compassionate to have said, 'Wolverhampton.'

'Geez, you'd notice the difference.'

'I'll say.'

But of course the one who was noticing the difference

was him. He had accosted me because he needed someone to talk to now that he'd finally made it after days of driving. He had to hear his own voice in Surfers just to be certain it was he who was here. He stood by my side, looking out over the untouched sand and the blinding sea. 'It's like bloody Hawaii,' he said at last. Then in case that gave me the wrong impression of him, in case I thought he was skiting, he added, 'Not that I've ever been to Hawaii, but I bet it's like this.'

There's no helping the poor. They just can't lie like the rich.

I asked him if he intended to stay long.

'Here? Might stay all summer. I've got nothing else to do. There's no work down there. That's why I came away. If I'm going to do nothing I thought I might as well do it up here.'

'No point in not staying, then,' I said.

He gave me the sad smile of the habitually isolated – wary but eager. He'd been on his own in his big, ugly, beaten-up Holden for days. Mine was the first non-radio voice he'd heard. I the only living soul he so far knew, in Surfers Paradise. I was only sorry that I couldn't, in my own person, encapsulate more that was paradisal for him.

I wished him well and watched him walk off towards the beach in his stained olive-green trousers – strides if ever I'd seen a pair – his silver buckle catching the sun. Directly in his path a young woman was coming out of the surf. Apart from a twist of string about her loins she was naked, and as she walked she shook the water from her breasts, droplet by droplet. He had his back to me now but I could see the tension of the long drive and the worry about unemployment flowing out of his shoulders.

We, on the other hand, were growing heavier with every kilometre. Somewhere in between the twin towns of Coolangatta and Tweed Heads we crossed the border into New South Wales. The grand, expensive-looking Services Club, at which Gene Pitney was currently appearing, provided our farewell glimpse of the mess that was Queensland morality; for it was to this club that Queenslanders trailed in their thousands after dark, to play the poker machines they were denied, for the good of their immortal souls, in their own state.

But that didn't mean we were pleased to leave it. 'Now that I'm in New South Wales I feel I'm safe,' Ros kept saying. 'I feel as though I'm home.'

I'd never heard the words 'safe' and 'home' sound so desolate.

READ MORE IN PENGUIN

For complete information about books available from Penguin and how to order them, please write to us at the appropriate address below. Please note that for copyright reasons the selection of books varies from country to country.

IN THE UNITED KINGDOM: Please write to *Dept. EP, Penguin Books Ltd, Bath Road, Harmondsworth, Middlesex UB7 0DA.*

IN THE UNITED STATES: Please write to *Consumer Sales, Penguin USA, P.O. Box 999, Dept. 17109, Bergenfield, New Jersey 07621-0120.* VISA and MasterCard holders call 1-800-253-6476 to order Penguin titles.

IN CANADA: Please write to *Penguin Books Canada Ltd, 10 Alcorn Avenue, Suite 300, Toronto, Ontario M4V 3B2.*

IN AUSTRALIA: Please write to *Penguin Books Australia Ltd, P.O. Box 257, Ringwood, Victoria 3134.*

IN NEW ZEALAND: Please write to *Penguin Books (NZ) Ltd, Private Bag 102902, North Shore Mail Centre, Auckland 10.*

IN INDIA: Please write to *Penguin Books India Pvt Ltd, 706 Eros Apartments, 56 Nehru Place, New Delhi 110 019.*

IN THE NETHERLANDS: Please write to *Penguin Books Netherlands bv, Postbus 3507, NL-1001 AH Amsterdam.*

IN GERMANY: Please write to *Penguin Books Deutschland GmbH, Metzlerstrasse 26, 60594 Frankfurt am Main.*

IN SPAIN: Please write to *Penguin Books S. A., Bravo Murillo 19, 1° B, 28015 Madrid.*

IN ITALY: Please write to *Penguin Italia s.r.l., Via Felice Casati 20, I-20124 Milano.*

IN FRANCE: Please write to *Penguin France S. A., 17 rue Lejeune, F-31000 Toulouse.*

IN JAPAN: Please write to *Penguin Books Japan, Ishikiribashi Building, 2-5-4, Suido, Bunkyo-ku, Tokyo 112.*

IN GREECE: Please write to *Penguin Hellas Ltd, Dimocritou 3, GR-106 71 Athens.*

IN SOUTH AFRICA: Please write to *Longman Penguin Southern Africa (Pty) Ltd, Private Bag X08, Bertsham 2013.*